AEI LEGISLATIVE ANALYSES
Balanced analyses of current proposals before the Congress, prepared with the help of specialists in law, economics, and government

Broadcast Deregulation

1985
99th Congress
1st Session

AMERICAN ENTERPRISE INSTITUTE
FOR PUBLIC POLICY RESEARCH
Washington, D.C.

ISBN 0-8447-0263-3
Legislative Analysis No. 48, 99th Congress
July 1985

Contents

1. Introduction 1
2. Comparative Renewal 2
   - Development of Present License Renewal Procedures.... 5
   - Recent Legislative Proposals 7
   - Arguments 10
3. Equal Access and the Fairness Doctrine 15
   - Equal Access 15
   - The Fairness Doctrine 16
   - Recent Proposals to Modify Equal Access and the Fairness Doctrine 18
   - Arguments 19

   Appendix 25

   Notes to Text 27

1
Introduction

Broadcast deregulation, a specific objective of the Federal Communications Commission (FCC) for the last several years, has impressively reduced FCC oversight of the internal affairs of broadcast stations. For instance, commercial television stations are no longer required to show on their applications for renewal that they have provided a minimum of 5 percent local, 5 percent informational, and 10 percent nonentertainment programming and are no longer required to ascertain the problems and needs of the local community being served by the station or to list the programs intended to treat those problems and needs.[1] Guidelines limiting the amount of commercial matter per hour to sixteen minutes have been eliminated.[2] Broadcasters are no longer required to maintain program logs listing all programs broadcast, as well as the program type and source.[3] Deregulation of radio broadcast stations has gone even further. Restrictions on ownership of broadcast stations have been eased. Controls over certain broadcast business practices have been eliminated or are being eliminated.[4]

These deregulatory initiatives draw on a new conception of public interest regulation, which holds that the public interest is best served by allowing market forces the fullest possible play. FCC regulators have stated their belief that the increasing amount of competition facing commercial broadcasting will provide incentives to ensure programming that responds to the needs of the community[5] and that, consequently, less intrusive controls will suffice to carry out the FCC's mandate of ensuring that the broadcast spectrum is allocated in accordance with the public interest.[6]

Despite this reduction in regulation, two major broadcast deregulation issues have not yet been resolved, although both the commission and Congress have given them extensive consideration. One issue is the revision of procedures for licensing and license renewal of broadcast stations. The present procedure requires a determination that license renewal is in the public interest. This determination is made on the basis of various factors relating to the broadcaster's service to the community in which the station is located, and it is open to participation by competing applicants. There is a broad consensus that some revision of the licensing procedures is appropriate, but the extent of the change is still controversial. A second major unresolved issue is elimination of the equal access provisions of the Communications Act and the related Fairness Doctrine requirements, which require broadcasters, if they provide certain types of coverage of political issues or other controversial issues of public importance, to provide coverage in a manner that affords an opportunity for equal coverage to advocates of opposing viewpoints. No consensus is emerging on what, if any, changes should be made in these provisions.

Both these issues have spawned extensive debate and many proposals for change. One reason these issues are difficult to resolve is that each has an inherent First Amendment problem. Thus the question concerning the comparative renewal process is twofold: Does the present renewal process take into account the public interest and the legitimate business interests of both the licensee and potential challengers in the allocation of spectrum space, and also does the process intrude upon licensees' freedom of expression by requiring the FCC to take into account, in determining whether to renew a license, the content of the licensee's broadcast programming? Similarly, with respect to equal access and the Fairness Doctrine, the question is not only whether or not the doctrine works (that is, whether it effectively increases the diversity and balance of opinions expressed on broadcast media), but if so whether it imposes restraints incompatible with the First Amendment on the broadcaster's freedom of expression.

The First Amendment arguments have gained strength in recent years because of changes in broadcast technology. The underlying justification for broadcast regulation is spectrum scarcity, and spectrum scarcity also provides the rationale for regulation of program content.[7] The proliferation of new telecommunications media over the past decade, however, has undermined the argument that spectrum scarcity justifies stringent regulation. The extent of recent changes is illustrated by a comparison between the number of broadcast outlets in operation when the contours of broadcast regulation were established and those in operation at present. When the Communications Act of 1934 was enacted, fewer than 900 radio stations and no television stations were on the air.[8] As of May 1985, there were 4,785 AM stations, 3,771 commercial FM stations, 1,194 educational FM stations, 907 commercial television stations, 184 educational UHF television stations and 115 educational VHF television stations.[9] The percentage of cities with multiple channels of television has grown exponentially.[10] Ninety-seven percent of U. S. households have televisions,[11] with at least 90 percent of American households receiving three or more over-the-air television signals and six or more radio signals.[12]

Proliferation of broadcast signals has not been the only change. Cable television systems now routinely offer twenty to fifty channels, and approximately 40 percent of television households now subscribe to cable.[13] In addition, the advent of cable, low power, and subscription television; direct broadcast satellites; satellite master antenna systems; multipoint distribution services; instructional television fixed-service stations; teletext; videotex; and fiber optics technology have opened up new communication outlets. Home telecommunications equipment is no longer limited to receiving a handful of broadcast stations, and the situation of scarcity, which provided the rationale for rejecting the First Amendment challenges to broadcast regulation in the early years of commercial broadcasting, has given way to a situation of abundance.[14]

Under these circumstances, have spectrum scarcity and consequent limits on the number of electronic "voices" that can be heard — the underlying rationale for much of broadcast regulation — diminished in importance? Should broadcasters still be held to a concept of community service detached from marketplace forces but enforced through the renewal process? Has the time come to allow market forces to determine spectrum allocation through auctioning of broadcast licenses? Has the technical transformation of the communciations industry in recent years strengthened broadcasters' First Amendment claims and enhanced the argument for elimination of content controls such as those represented by the equal access provisions and the Fairness Doctrine? Does the economic power of broadcast stations, particularly television stations, provide an alternative basis for content regulation that is adequate by constitutional standards? Are the distinctions between print and broadcast media that have historically been relied upon to justify greater regulation of broadcast media still constitutionally adequate in view of changing technology? These questions will be addressed below.

2
COMPARATIVE RENEWAL

The question of reforming the broadcast license renewal process has provoked extensive legislative interest. Under current law, the FCC issues broadcast licenses on the basis of its determination that the public interest, convenience, and necessity will be served by issuance of the license.[15] In making this public interest determination, the FCC looks to whether or not issue of the license will promote diversification of control of the media of mass communications; whether or not the owners of the stations are involved full-time in station operation; the nature of proposed program services; the past broadcast record of the applicants; the most efficient use of the frequency; and the character of the applicants. These factors are reviewed not only with respect to the application of a licensee who is applying for renewal but also to any competing applications filed by a new applicant for the license. It has long been held that the Communications Act requires a full comparative evaluation of a challenger's license application.[16]

There are two much debated problems with respect to this license renewal process. The first is a practical problem. When a broadcaster seeks renewal of a license, he has an investment in the community and a record of service to the community, which gives rise to an expectation that the license will be renewed. That some degree of renewal expectancy is permissible has long been held.[17] It has also been held, however, that the renewal expectancy may not be raised to "an irrebuttable presumption in favor of the incumbent."[18] Broadcasters assert that the comparative hearing leaves them vulnerable to a form of blackmail in which a competing application is filed, without a reasonable expectation that it will be granted, merely to trigger a comparative hearing. Broadcasters have long argued that the statute should be revised to provide for a comparative hearing only when the commission has already determined that the incumbent's license should not be renewed.

The second problem again places in sharp focus the First Amendment problems inherent in broadcast regulation. The problem is whether this governmental supervision of programming decisions is compatible with the First Amendment, particularly when the underlying rationale of spectrum scarcity is no longer as compelling as it once was. In determining whether a license should be renewed, the commission gives substantial weight to the program service that the license applicant has provided and intends to provide. Early in the history of broadcast regulation, the Supreme Court was asked to consider whether the public interest standard in the Communications Act provision on licensing allowed the commission to consider the program services to be offered as well as the technical capabilities of the broadcaster. The Supreme Court upheld the FCC's assertion of a broad interpretation of the statute against challenges based on the First Amendment as well as arguments in favor of a narrow interpretation of the statutory mandate.[19] The Court explained that the "public interest" to be served under the Communications Act is the interest of the listening public in "the larger and more effective use" of broadcast facilities.[20] The underlying justification for this broad interpretation of the public interest language was spectrum scarcity. Because "natural factors" limited the number of radio stations that could be licensed, the FCC concluded and the Supreme Court confirmed that the FCC could legitimately choose between applicants upon the basis of criteria that took program content into account. The Supreme Court explained that the FCC had to have some power to foster greater program diversity instead of being limited to the engineering and technical aspects of radio regulation.[21] Consequently, in making licensing decisions the FCC was not limited to considering only the engineering and technical merits of various applications. This latitude was reaffirmed by the Court in 1969 in *Red Lion Broadcasting v. FCC*.[22]

DEVELOPMENT OF PRESENT LICENSE RENEWAL PROCEDURES

Current license renewal procedures have been shaped by a tug-of-war among Congress, the FCC, and the courts reflecting the tension between statutory requirements, which broadcasters find extremely burdensome; the broad interpretation of the statutory terms, which the courts have endorsed and the commission has sometimes followed and sometimes ignored; and the pervasive question of whether the FCC's broad interpretation of the public interest infringes upon the First Amendment. The most controversial question with respect to the criteria to be used is what weight should be given to the incumbent license holder's renewal expectation, which of course is closely related to the licensee's record of service to the community.

The comparative criteria that the FCC will apply to license applications were spelled out in a 1965 policy statement.[23] This policy statement covered hearings involving competing applicants for a new station, although the FCC later stated that the same comparative criteria set out in the policy statement (if not the weight assigned to each such criterion) must be considered in renewal hearings.[24] In 1969 the FCC applied the comparative criteria in the first of only two cases in the history of broadcasting in which an incumbent, station WHDH in Boston, lost its license as a result of a comparative renewal proceeding.[25] In WHDH, the FCC stated its intention to ensure that "the foundations for determining the best practicable service, as between a renewal and a new applicant, are more nearly equal at their outset."[26] This decision created much anxiety among broadcasters, who feared that the stability of the industry would be threatened by license renewal challenges.[27]

The reaction to the WHDH decision led immediately to congressional action and, one year later, to an FCC policy statement. The congressional action was the introduction of S. 2004,[28] a bill that would have prohibited the commission from considering competing applications for a license at renewal time unless it had first found, based on the licensee's renewal application, that a grant of the licensee's application would not be in the public interest, convenience, or necessity. Although the bill originally had a great deal of support, it came under increasing attack by citizen groups while action on the bill was delayed by other matters. In early 1970, while S. 2004 was still under consideration but chances for its passage seemed remote, the FCC issued a policy statement.[29] The commission stated that license renewal would be granted, and competing applications dismissed, if the incumbent's program service during the past license term was found to have been "substantially attuned" to local interests and needs.[30] The sponsor of S. 2004, Senator John Pastore (D-R.I.), issued a statement that his subcommittee would not take any further action on S. 2004 until the FCC's policy had a fair test.[31] The following year, however, the U. S. Court of Appeals for the D. C. Circuit invalidated the FCC's policy as enunciated in the policy statement because it deprived competing applicants of their Section 309(e) right to a full comparative hearing.[32] In the opinion, Judge Wright characterized the policy statement as an attempt to enact S. 2004 administratively. He did, however, allow for some preference to existing licensees by commenting that "superior performance should be a plus of major significance in renewal proceedings."[33]

As a result of *Citizens' Communications,* the commission returned to applying its 1965 policy statement on comparative criteria to license renewal challenges.[34] In applying the policy, the commission emphasized past broadcast service and virtually assured license renewal to an incumbent who showed substantial, meritorious, or superior service to the public.[35] In 1974 Congress took action again in an attempt to clarify the standards for license renewal. The House and Senate overwhelmingly passed slightly different versions of a bill that extended broadcast license terms and provided for a two-step renewal process as originally proposed in S. 2004.[36] This process would have required the FCC to examine the incumbent's record first and deny renewal before considering any new applicants. The 93rd Congress adjourned without passage of this legislation because of a disagreement over the length of the new broadcast license terms.[37]

Meanwhile, the renewal application of Cowles Florida Broadcasting was under consideration by the commission. The administrative law judge held hearings and granted Cowles's renewal on the basis of its "thoroughly acceptable" past broadcast record, even though the competing applicant fared better under the diversification and integration comparative criteria. On appeal, the commission first affirmed and then modified the judge's decision but allowed Cowles's license renewal.[38]

In September 1978, the U. S. Court of Appeals for the D. C. Circuit vacated the FCC's decision in favor of Cowles, finding that the commission had acted unreasonably and without substantial record support in preferring the renewal application.[39] It found that the FCC had "practically erected a presumption of renewal that is inconsistent with the full hearing requirement of §309(e)."[40] The court remanded the case for further proceedings and directed the FCC to explain more intelligibly the manner in which the incumbent's past performance should be integrated into the comparative analysis. A revised opinion suggested that "meritorious" service could give an incumbent an advantage in a comparative proceeding.[41] On remand, the FCC again voted in favor of Cowles on the basis of the station's past service, indicating that a renewal expectancy is necessary in the interests of industry stability where meritorious service has been provided.[42] On appeal, the Court of Appeals upheld the FCC policy that renewal expectancy is a factor to be weighted with all other factors and that the better the past record, the greater the renewal expectancy weight.[43]

As a consequence of all of these decisions, the precise weight to be accorded the incumbent's record and the renewal expectancy based thereon is quite unsettled.

RECENT LEGISLATIVE PROPOSALS

In the 99th Congress, the principal bill to date concerning broadcast license renewal is H. R. 1977, introduced April 3, 1985, by Representatives Thomas J. Tauke (R-Iowa) and W. J. Tauzin (D-La.), with forty-four cosponsors. This bill is identical to one introduced by Representatives Tauke and Tauzin in the 98th Congress.[44] H. R. 1977 provides that the FCC, in acting on a license renewal application, may not consider the application of any other person for the facilities for which renewal is sought. The bill also modifies the petition to deny process (which allows a member of the public to petition for license denial where the licensee has not lived up to public interest obligations) to make that process available as a further check on licensee responsiveness to community needs. The bill endorses recent FCC deregulatory initiatives.

Revisions in the Renewal Process. H. R. 1977 allows an automatic grant of an application for renewal unless the commission finds that the actions of the licensee evidenced such serious disregard for the provisions of the Communications Act and the rules and policies of the commission to justify the denial of the application.

The revisions in the renewal process proposed in H. R. 1977 should be compared with those proposed in H. R. 6122 in the 98th Congress. While eliminating the comparative renewal process, H. R. 6122 would have continued and elaborated upon public interest requirements. Under H. R. 6122, the commission would grant the renewal application of any television licensee if it found that the licensee had addressed the problems, needs, and interests of children, minorities, elderly individuals, and other residents of the service area. The bill directed the FCC to establish requirements specifying minimum amounts of local programs; informational programs; and programs aimed at children, minorities, and the elderly; and it would have established a rating system based on the amount of such programming the station provided. Stations would have been required to maintain sufficient records of such public interest programming to indicate compliance with these quantitative standards. In addition to these requirements, licensees could not have seriously violated the rules, regulations, or policies of the act nor could they have committed minor violations of the act which, taken together, would constitute a pattern of abuse.

The renewal provisions in these bills illustrate that although many people agree that the comparative renewal process should be modified, no one agrees about the form the changes should take. H. R. 1977 and H. R. 6122 would both eliminate the comparative renewal process that broadcasters have found so threatening. The renewal standards proposed in the two bills differ substantially, however. The relatively simple showing that a renewal applicant would have to make under H. R. 1977 contrasts with the detailed quantification standards the applicant would have to satisfy under H. R. 6122.

Under H. R. 1977, the FCC would have to grant the application for the renewal of a license unless it found that the actions of the licensee evidenced such disregard for the provisions of the act and FCC rules and policies as to justify denial. This policy would ensure automatic renewal for a licensee who has complied with Fairness Doctrine obligations, technical regulations, interference prohibitions, or rules against broadcast of obscenities, for example, without taking programming decisions into account.

H. R. 6122 requires both radio and television broadcasters to address local needs but also to take into account children, minority groups, and the elderly. That bill also quantifies the public interest standard by requiring the commission to establish minimum amounts of local and informational programming and programming aimed at children, minorities, and the elderly. If such a quantification standard were adopted, broadcasters would still have to abide by other FCC rules and regulations for their licenses to be renewed. Thus, a licensee who has provided the minimum public interest programming required but has failed to fulfill his Fairness Doctrine obligations or has ignored other FCC policies would not have his application automatically granted.[45]

Revisions of the Petition to Deny Process. H. R. 1977 contains provisions modifying the Section 309 procedure by which persons may file petitions to deny the application of a licensee seeking renewal. Under this bill, a petition to deny would be subject to an initial FCC review to determine whether the applicant had made out a prima facie case. The license applicant would reply to the petition only if the FCC determined that the petitioner had made out such a case. The bill would allow the FCC, after review of the petition and any responses thereto, to deny either the license application or the petition to deny if it found that the petition raised no substantial and material questions of fact. H. R. 1977 also requires that, if the FCC finds a substantial and material question of fact and holds a hearing, it must do so expeditiously and render a decision within 180 days. In such a hearing, the burden of proof would always be upon the petitioner, and the burden of proceeding with the introduction of evidence would be upon the petitioner unless the FCC ordered otherwise.

Again, the provisions of H. R. 1977 should be compared with those of H. R. 6122. The provisions of H. R. 6122 pertaining to the petition to deny procedure would afford more participation by the petitioner than does current law. The bill would allow a petitioner to request that the FCC conduct a thorough investigation into the matter before it, or provide reasonable opportunity and means for the petitioner to do so, except under certain circumstances. Section 309(d) would also be amended to allow the petitioner to have "meaningful participation" in any such investigation. This bill also would render unlawful any agreement made without FCC approval to pay money in exchange for withdrawal of a petition to deny. This provision is similar to the current Section 311 requirement that the FCC may not approve a settlement agreement for withdrawal of a competing application if the application was filed for the purpose of obtaining a settlement.[46]

Arguments

Although a broad consensus seems to support the proposition that broadcast licensing procedures should be revised, no consensus exists on how far those revisions should go. Most people apparently agree that in renewal situations an incumbent should not be subjected to a full comparative hearing unless the incumbent has been shown unqualified for renewal. No consensus exists, however, on whether the broadcaster should still have to demonstrate at license renewal time compliance with the same public interest standards that traditionally have been used.

The strongest stand in favor of continued use of a public interest standard is found in the quantification proposal.[47] Opponents of quantification argue that any law quantifying public interest standards in this manner infringes upon broadcasters' First Amendment rights by regulating programming content and is especially egregious if the standards are set too high.[48] Broadcasters want to retain the power to use their independent judgment as journalists and programmers without having the government question their decisions. They also contend that if the standards are set too low, the effect will be negative. Percentages or point minimums will act as a floor *and* a ceiling for public interest programming because economic facts may discourage the licensee from providing more than the minimum required. Opponents of quantification also criticize the quantification standard for its inflexibility: it assumes that the program needs of the public are identical in all communities.

Proponents of the quantification standard see it as less intrusive than the present system. Under the present system a broadcaster is judged after the fact on his performance. Under a quantified standard, broadcasters would know what is expected of them; and, if they fulfill the requirements, they could be assured of renewal. Proponents do not agree that the standard is inflexible but rather characterize it as a point system that gives broadcasters the flexibility to choose what kind of public interest programs to air and when to air them. Properly formulated, the quantification standard can give broadcasters the flexibility to vary programming based on local market conditions.

Proponents of repealing the comparative renewal process urge that it is a costly, time-consuming, and burdensome process that produces no benefit to the public. The original purpose of allowing competing applicants to challenge a broadcaster's license was to create a competitive environment that would stimulate licensees to provide better service to the public.[49] Proponents of repeal urge that comparative renewal is not a proper way to achieve these intended objectives and that other means, such as the petition to deny process and the competitive marketplace, are more effective. The lengthy and costly hearings divert the resources of both the industry and the government away from the objective of providing better broadcast service. Representative James T. Broyhill (R-N.C.) stated in hearings held before the House Subcommittee on Telecommunications, Consumer Protection, and Finance on September 19, 1984, that a recent survey by the National Association of Broadcasters demonstrated that broadcasters whose licenses are challenged spend an average of $830,000 in legal fees related to the comparative hearing process. When a station that is being challenged is serving its community well by providing public affairs programming or otherwise addressing the needs and interests of the listening audience, subjecting it to the process of defending its record in a comparative renewal proceeding is unfair.

Proponents urge that the performance of the licensee in the operation of the station, rather than non-performance-related criteria such as diversification and integration, should be the focus of renewal procedures.[50] They contend that the current procedure of comparing the promises of a challenger with the actual service record of an incumbent licensee is an impossible task.[51] The burden in such a proceeding is essentially upon the incumbent licensee because it must defend its day-to-day operating decisions made over a period of time, while the challenger need only submit an application designed to fare well under the comparative criteria. The process is viewed as one more example of regulatory intrusion into the licensee's programming decisions because of the kind of detailed analysis required by the comparative renewal process. This intrusion is inconsistent with the FCC's professed belief in freedom of the press and free speech.[52]

Advocates of repeal contend that the current system creates instability in the broadcast industry. Broadcasters invest large sums of money in the construction and operation of stations. If broadcasters are not assured automatic license renewal after having expended much energy and money toward providing high quality service, large operations could be wiped out on the basis of a competing applicant's promise to provide better service. This threat, repeal advocates contend, makes it more difficult for broadcasters to serve their communities. Rather than requiring private businesses to defend their licenses continually, the government should tell incumbents exactly what it expects of them; and if they fulfill these expectations, it should renew their licenses.

The objective of the comparative renewal process when originally created was to spur competition. Repeal advocates argue that marketplace forces provide this competitive spur, causing broadcasters to work harder to provide better service. This competitive environment among existing licensees, not a competitive environment created by the threat of a challenger at license renewal time, forces broadcasters to provide high quality programming.[53] Thus the comparative renewal process is not an effective means of obtaining the intended objective.

Critics also argue that the current system provides no threshold procedural standard for challenges to a license. Challenges are too easily initiated and are thus subject to abuse without any corresponding benefit to the public. Such abuses include the filing of challenges for the sole purpose of obtaining a settlement in exchange for withdrawal of the application. This action has been characterized by Representative Tauzin as putting the public interest up for sale.[54]

Proponents of repeal assert that although comparative renewal does afford a forum to discuss shortcomings in licensee performance, the petition to deny process remains available and is equally effective.

Some advocates of eliminating comparative renewal contend that the current petition to deny process protects the public interest and poses less of a threat to the broadcasting industry than does comparative renewal. The petition gives the public the opportunity to object to license renewal of a station that is ignoring the community's needs and interests or is otherwise performing poorly. Repeal advocates urge that petitions to deny are just as effective as comparative renewal in exposing a station that is guilty of a pattern of serious wrongdoing or has failed to supply a reasonable amount of nonentertainment programming.

Some proponents of ending comparative renewal urge that the petition to deny process would be made easier if comparative renewal were eliminated. One dispute is whether or not a petitioner should be able to obtain discovery before the commission decides if a hearing is necessary. Currently a petitioner must make a prima facie showing that granting a license renewal would be inconsistent with the public interest. A provision in H. R. 6122 would allow the petitioner to request discovery or conduct discovery himself before a hearing is set, but it also provides that no discovery could be taken if (1) the petitioner failed to provide specific evidence sufficient to place the commission on notice that a factual uncertainty may exist regarding the basis for license renewal, and (2) the circumstances indicated that the commission has no need for additional information to make an informed decision.

Citizen groups and others who are critical of the move to repeal the comparative renewal process contend that the process does in fact stimulate higher quality performance by broadcasters. If incumbents know that their licenses will not automatically be renewed unless they exhibit a level of service to the community to enable them to defeat a challenger, they will not strive to achieve that level. Achievement does not come from an environment of contentment. Ensuring automatic license renewal will only perpetuate the broadcasters' belief that they have a vested property interest in their frequencies and that they retain this interest in perpetuity. Critics of repeal argue that the marketplace does not provide the incentive to avoid inferior performance in the same way that the comparative renewal process does. As an example of the failure of the marketplace to spur competitive programming, they point to the lack of programming aimed at children, minorities, and the elderly, even in areas served by a multitude of stations where competition for listeners is fierce.

Opponents of repeal urge that the comparative renewal process is not as much of a burden as some claim. Only two stations in the history of broadcasting have ever lost their licenses to a challenger;[55] full comparative renewal proceedings have been estimated at an average of one television and two radio license comparative renewals per year over the past twenty years.[56] Considering that currently more than 9,000 radio stations and more than 1,000 television stations exist, opponents of repeal suggest that the threat posed by the comparative renewal process is minuscule and the industry claims of instability and uncertainty are exaggerated. In response to the argument that the process poses a threat to the stability of the broadcast industry, opponents of repeal point to the financial success of the industry today. Finally, opponents urge that the abuse of the comparative renewal process is minimal compared with the benefits it produces. Because of the high cost of pursuing a license challenge, few competitors would likely challenge any but the most minimal performers. As for applicants who file competing applications for the purpose of obtaining a settlement, such settlements will not be approved by the FCC under the mandate of Section 311(c)(3).[57] One has no reason to suppose that the FCC is unable to determine when an application is filed for the purpose of obtaining a settlement for withdrawing the application.

Some citizen groups claim that the comparative renewal process is crucial to ensure that minorities have access to ownership of stations. In comparative hearings for new licenses, the preference given to minorities has become the single most effective mechanism to promote minority ownership of broadcast stations.[58] Although minorities have not gained licenses by challenging any incumbents in license renewal proceedings, the possibility should not be cut off by repeal.

Finally, repeal opponents urge that the existing system offers minimal governmental intrusion.[59] An incumbent and a prospective licensee are essentially involved in a private suit when they are in a comparative renewal proceeding. The challenger is a private party that has committed its resources to vindicate the public interest in providing better programming. The only other method of challenging a license, the petition-to-deny procedure, requires the government to make value judgments and to reject a licensee based on the content of the licensee's broadcast; but in a comparative renewal proceeding, the FCC chooses — without rendering a judgment on program content — someone who can better serve the listening audience.[60]

An alternative to comparative renewal, though it has not yet received widespread administrative or legislative consideration, is to treat the spectrum as a publicly owned resource that will be made temporarily available by auction to the highest bidder.[61] The advantages of such a proposal are many. As a practical matter, sale of spectrum space would provide a relatively simple and easily administered criterion for allocation and would avoid entirely the administrative thicket of comparative renewal. Auction would allow market allocation of spectrum space, historically the most efficient allocation method for scarce resources. At the same time, it would supply a new revenue source. If the spectrum were allocated by auction, those constraints upon broadcasters' First Amendment rights that result from public interest regulation of broadcast content would be terminated.

The difficulty with going to a system of spectrum allocated by auction is building a consensus in favor of a complete break of the association between spectrum allocation and public interest regulation of broadcasters.

3
EQUAL ACCESS AND THE FAIRNESS DOCTRINE

EQUAL ACCESS

The legislative mandate for equal access is found in Section 315 of the Communications Act.[62] Section 315 provides:

> If any licensee shall permit any person who is a legally qualified candidate for any public office to use a broadcasting station, he shall afford equal opportunities to all other such candidates for that office in the use of such broadcast stations.

This provision was in the act as passed in 1934. Amendments in 1959 provided certain exceptions for appearances by candidates on bona fide newscasts, news interviews, news documentaries, and on-the-spot coverage of bona fide news events. Section 315 is supplemented by FCC rules and explained in FCC publications.[63]

This section applies only to legally qualified candidates for public office. The FCC's implementing regulations contain a detailed definition of who is to be regarded as a legally qualified candidate,[64] set out what charges may be made for use of stations by legally qualified candidates under this section,[65] forbid discrimination between legally qualified candidates with respect to access to the broadcast facility, require licensees to keep records of requests for political broadcast time, and require equal time requests to be submitted within certain periods.[66] The ultimate penalty for failure to comply with the rules is revocation of the station license.[67]

The section applies only to use of a broadcast station by a candidate. The term *use* has been subject to extensive interpretation in this context. Aside from the news exceptions of Section 315(a), most appearances by a candidate are considered uses within the meaning of the statute; even a nonpolitical appearance constitutes a use. In the case of spot advertising, if a candidate makes any appearance in which he or she is identified or identifiable by voice or picture, the whole announcement will be considered a use.[68] When a licensee airs a program about a political candidate, the program constitutes a use.[69]

Because the law requires equal treatment of opposing candidates, a licensee who sells time to supporters of a candidate who urge the candidate's election, discuss the campaign issues, or criticizes an opponent must be willing to sell comparable time to the spokesperson for an opponent. If the licensee gives free time to one such spokesperson, he or she must give free time to the other but need not afford free time in response to a paid program.[70] Licensees may not deny use of the station on the grounds that they believe the candidate has little or no chance of being nominated or elected or that there are too many candidates running for a particular office.[71]

The Fairness Doctrine

Besides setting out the equal access principle, Section 315 cautions that the equal access rules do not relieve broadcasters from "the obligation imposed upon them under this Act to operate in the public interest and to afford reasonable opportunity for the discussion of conflicting views on issues of public importance." This is a statutory acknowledgment of the FCC-developed Fairness Doctrine, the authority for which was originally derived from the general "public interest" standard of the Communications Act and the basic premises of which were first set forth in the commission's 1949 "Report on Editorializing."[72] In that report the commission noted that it had required broadcast licensees to allow a percentage of broadcast time for "the presentation of news and programs devoted to the consideration and discussion of public issues of interest in the community served by the particular station."[73] The commission referred to "the paramount right of the public in a free society to be informed and to have presented to it for acceptance or rejection the different attitudes and viewpoints . . . which are held by the various groups which make up the community"[74] and stated that to require broadcasters to present contrasting views on public issues was "within both the spirit and the letter of the First Amendment."[75]

Key concepts under the Fairness Doctrine are controversiality and public importance, and the FCC has developed guidelines to assist broadcasters in determining whether an issue is both controversial and of public importance.[76] A controversial issue is an issue that is the subject of vigorous debate, with substantial elements of the community in opposition to one another. Whether an issue is of public importance is determined by reviewing the amount of media coverage the issue has received; the degree of attention the issue has received from government officials and other community leaders; and, most important, the effect the issue will likely have on the community. The commission has stated that broadcasters can make these judgments only on a case-by-case basis and that the commission's role is limited to review, with heavy reliance on judgments of the licensees' reasonable good faith.[77]

Once an issue has been determined controversial and of public importance, the broadcaster must afford a reasonable opportunity for the discussion of conflicting viewpoints with respect to that issue. In determining whether a reasonable opportunity has been afforded, a broadcaster must consider (1) the total time allowed each view; (2) the frequency of announcements or programs afforded to the differing views; and (3) the relative size of the audience when announcements or programs are broadcast.[78] Broadcasters are not required to devote equal time to the discussion of opposing views, although the FCC will take into account that factor in determining reasonableness.

The licensee's duty to afford reasonable opportunity for presentation of contrasting viewpoints includes a duty to play a "conscious and positive role in encouraging the presentation of opposing viewpoints."[79] This duty requires the licensee to take affirmative steps toward finding a spokesperson for an opposing viewpoint.[80] For instance, when licensees have chosen to broadcast a controversial issue on a sponsored program or paid commercial advertisement and have been unable to obtain paid sponsorship for an opposing viewpoint, they must provide a forum for expression of opposing viewpoints at their own expense.[81] This means that they must give free airtime to a spokesperson whose organization cannot afford to pay for airtime if they have been unable to find someone who can pay. Furthermore, if such programming is unavailable from any other source, the broadcaster must initiate such programming.[82]

The commission leaves to the the broadcaster's discretion the selection of spokespersons and formats for presentation of contrasting views. Presentation of an opposing viewpoint, however, should be by persons who genuinely believe in what they are saying. The licensee cannot present a contrasting viewpoint in a bland, nonpartisan manner.

The FCC has promulgated regulations on two specific aspects of the Fairness Doctrine: personal attacks and political editorials.[83] The personal attack rules provide that the licensee has certain responsibilities when, during the presentation of views on a controversial issue of public importance, an attack is made upon the honesty, character, integrity, or like personal qualities of an unidentified person or group. When such an attack occurs, the licensee must, within a week, send to the persons or group attacked a notice that the broadcast took place and a script or tape or accurate summary of the attack and an offer of a reasonable opportunity to respond over the broadcast station.[84]

The political editorial rules provide that when a licensee in an editorial endorses or opposes a legally qualified candidate, the licensee has twenty-four hours after the editorial to transmit certain materials to opposing candidates or other qualified candidates for the same office. The materials must include a notice concerning the editorial, a script or a tape of the editorial, and an offer of reasonable opportunity to respond over the licensee's facilities. When editorials are broadcast too close to the election to allow these procedures to take place after the broadcast, the licensee must comply sufficiently in advance of the broadcast to enable the candidate to have an opportunity to make a timely response.[85]

RECENT PROPOSALS TO MODIFY EQUAL ACCESS AND THE FAIRNESS DOCTRINE

Legislative Proposals. A bill to repeal Section 315 and abolish the Fairness Doctrine has been introduced in the 99th Congress. S. 1038, introduced by Senator Robert Packwood (R-Ore.) on May 1, 1985, and cosponsored by Senator Barry Goldwater (R-Ariz.) (the "Freedom of Expression Act of 1985") would repeal Section 315 and remove the provision in Section 312(a) that provides that the commission may revoke any station license or construction permit for willful or repeated failure to allow a candidate for federal office reasonable access to the broadcasting station. S. 1038 also would strengthen the Communications Act's "no censorship" provision and would prohibit the commission from promulgating any regulation along the lines of the Equal Access and Fairness Doctrine provisions.

A bill similar to S. 1038 — S. 1917 — received serious consideration in the 98th Congress. Hearings were held before the Senate Committee on Commerce, Science, and Transportation in January and February 1984.[86] The committee considered the bill in June 1984, but despite revisions that would have made the bill apply only to radio and only for a five-year experimental period, the committee rejected the bill. Although the bill was supported by the National Association of Broadcasters, powerful opposition arose in both the Senate and the House.

Two other legislative proposals on equal access and the Fairness Doctrine have been introduced in the 99th Congress. Senator William Proxmire (D-Wisc.) has introduced S. 22 (the "First Amendment Clarification Act of 1985"), which would abolish both equal access and the Fairness Doctrine. S. 22, which is identical to legislation introduced by Senator Proxmire in 1975, 1977, 1979, 1981, and 1983,[87] states that the term "public interest, convenience and necessity" as used in the Communications Act "may not be construed to give the Commission jurisdiction to require the provision of broadcast time to any person or for the expression of any viewpoint."[88] S. 22 also eliminates the FCC authority to revoke the license of any station that refuses or fails to allow a candidate to buy broadcast time. The bill repeals Section 315 and removes certain restrictions on educational programming. The bill has been assigned to the Senate Committee on Commerce, Science, and Transportation. The second bill, H. R. 1570, introduced by Representative Robert L. Livingston (R-La.), provides that broadcast licensees may not refuse to sell advertising time for the broadcast of editorial advertisements but are not otherwise required to provide time for presentation of opposing views. The bill has been assigned to the House Committee on Energy and Commerce.

FCC Proposal to Modify the Fairness Doctrine. Although the origin of equal access is clearly statutory, the origin of the Fairness Doctrine is partly statutory and partly a product of the FCC's interpretation of its mandate to regulate in the public interest. The FCC has recently raised the question of whether or not the statutory language endorsing the Fairness Doctrine, which was added to Section 315 in 1959, was intended merely to inform the commission that Congress did not regard the newly created news exemptions (also added in 1959) as incompatible with the Fairness Doctrine.[89] This interpretation would support an argument that Congress by these amendments to the act did not remove the commission's discretion to modify the Fairness Doctrine if, in the light of changing circumstances, such a modification became desirable.

ARGUMENTS

The purpose of the First Amendment is to preserve an uninhibited marketplace of ideas.[90] The First Amendment right associated with broadcast communication has been held to be the right of the public to have access to a multitude of viewpoints on issues of public importance. The Supreme Court stated in *Red Lion* v. *FCC* that "it is the right of the viewers and listeners, not the right of the broadcasters, which is paramount. . . . It is the right of the public to receive suitable access to social, political, esthetic, moral, and other ideas and experiences which is crucial here."[91] Toward this end, regulation of the content of broadcast communication generally is forbidden.[92]

Do Equal Access and the Fairness Doctrine Impermissibly Regulate the Content of Broadcast Communication? Proponents of repeal of Section 315 contend that these provisions impermissibly control the content of broadcast communication by interfering with the broadcaster's decision to make editorial statements on controversial issues of public importance and by requiring broadcasters to provide certain kinds of coverage even though they may not agree with the viewpoint expressed. Proponents of repeal argue that these aspects of equal access and the Fairness Doctrine constitute a severe threat to the First Amendment rights of journalists by dictating what a broadcaster must put on the air and by allowing government interference in areas that were intended to be free from intrusion. According to this viewpoint, that the intentions of the regulators are pure makes no difference; the result is still substitution of government choice for editorial discretion.

Opponents of repeal say that is not the result. What a broadcaster may or may not say is not specifically restricted. The statute does not prevent the broadcaster from airing any programs or advertisements, nor does it censor the contents of any broadcast. The broadcaster retains the freedom and flexibility of choosing the amount of time to be given to an opposing viewpoint, the person who will speak, and the format of the program. The broadcaster is not bound under the Fairness Doctrine to afford equal time or to afford time on the same program to discussion of opposing views. Those who oppose repeal of Section 315 argue that because the statute requires more speech rather than restricting speech, it does not impose an unreasonable burden on broadcasters and does not infringe upon their First Amendment rights to determine the content of their programs.

If the Statute Does Regulate Content, What Is Its Justification? Clearly the First Amendment forbids content regulation for print communications media. The First Amendment forbids such regulation even though newspapers are powerful shapers of public opinion. The Supreme Court held in *Miami Herald Co.* v. *Tornillo*[93] that any right-to-access statute is flatly unconstitutional if applied to newspapers. Yet content regulation of broadcast media through Section 315 is justified by the power that the broadcast media exercise over public opinion.[94]

Another argument propounded by the courts in upholding content regulation of the broadcast media is that equal access and the Fairness Doctrine foster public discussion by providing access to all views and candidates. Yet, in admonishing against regulation of newspapers, the Supreme Court noted in *New York Times* v. *Sullivan* that the "government enforced right of access inescapably dampens the vigor and limits the variety of public debate."[95] Proponents of repeal of Section 315 argue that this statement is equally applicable to the electronic media. They argue that once the current requirements are removed and broadcasters are given First Amendment parity with print journalists, they will feel freer to air controversial topics and provide public discussion of issues.

At bottom, the rationale for content control over broadcast media and not over print media goes back to spectrum scarcity. No one needs a license to put ideas down on paper and to distribute them; newsprint is not a public resource. Anyone who wants to print a leaflet or newspaper advocating a point of view or supporting a candidate may do so. The airwaves, however, are a public resource and only a select few are granted licenses.

This situation requires those who are granted the temporary privilege of use of the airwaves to act in the public interest in making sure that issues are presented fairly. A station that broadcasts one side of an issue or covers the campaign of only one candidate does a disservice to those members of the listening public who want to make informed decisions.

This argument is attenuated by the new array of telecommunication media that are now available. The argument is further attenuated by the blurred distinction between print and electronic media. Critics of the Fairness Doctrine argue that when jointly owned newspapers and radio stations use verbatim copies of each other's news stories, to subject the radio station's broadcast of the news and not the newspaper's printed version to government regulation does not make sense. The distinction between the print and electronic media becomes less defined when airwaves are used to transmit copy for newspaper editions across the country. For instance, the *Wall Street Journal* is transmitted by satellite to a printing plant in Dallas where it is printed for the middle west.[96] Some newspapers transmit print via teletext to home television sets.[97] Thus, the argument goes, with the blurring of the boundary between print and electronic media, regulating one and not the other also does not make sense.

Is Section 315 Effective in Promoting the Goal of Increasing Public Access to a Diverse Flow of Information? Several points support the argument that Section 315 actually stifles debate on controversial issues and prevents the public from being fully informed. First, Section 315 provides an economic disincentive to air controversial issues. This disincentive arises because broadcasters who provide coverage of controversial issues may be required to give free airtime to someone who wants to voice an opposing viewpoint or may be obliged to reject a paying advertiser for fear broadcast of the advertisement may trigger equal time requirements for persons who have no resources to pay. Even if a spokesperson is able to pay for the airtime, the opposing viewpoint may cause indirect financial loss through disruption of the regular programming schedule.

Second, compliance with the equal access provisions and the Fairness Doctrine is administratively complex. Broadcasters contend that, because of the complexity of the requirements, station operators have difficulty telling when they are required to provide airtime for opposing viewpoints. For instance, commercials that contain statements that may be deemed a presentation of a viewpoint on an issue, even if merely presenting the advertiser's operations in a favorable light, present a situation where Section 315 might be triggered.[98] Similarly, broadcasters object to the burden placed upon them to determine who is a "legally qualified candidate" for public office to ascertain whether the candidate's appearance would trigger a right by other candidates to appear on the station. When multiple candidates stand for office, each potential candidate's status must be determined to ascertain whether he or she has a right to equal access. This time-consuming process provides a disincentive to put the candidates on the air. When many candidates run for an office, a station that cannot afford to provide airtime at the lowest unit charge to all of them may refuse to provide airtime to any. Another example arises when the licensee is unsure whether coverage of a candidate falls under a news exception or constitutes a use under the act. The broadcaster may refrain from covering the candidate to avoid the possibility of triggering an obligation to provide airtime to any other candidate who wishes to be heard.

Third, whenever broadcasters who have exercised their editorial judgment are confronted by persons who assert that an issue of public importance has been broadcast and who claim a right to air time, a broadcaster who disagrees may incur tremendous costs in defending his or her decision. Once they have encountered such a situation, broadcasters are less likely to air potentially controversial programs or commercials again.[99]

Fourth, these provisions are subject to abuse. For instance, if a group taking one side of an issue buys advertising time, an opposing group may spend all of its money on newspaper, billboard, and direct mail advertising instead of air time and then demand free air time of the station to voice its opposition because it cannot afford to pay. Because a broadcaster is required to air opposing viewpoints, the station must afford some free air time to the organization or run its own opposing statement. The doctrine does not require the station to put that particular organization's spokesperson on the air, however, nor does it require equality of exposure of the contrasting view. The FCC addressed this problem in 1974 and concluded that it is more important that the public have the opportunity to receive contrasting views than that the doctrine be abandoned because of the possible practices of a few parties.[100]

Supporters of the equal access provisions and the Fairness Doctrine contend that Section 315 is effective in promoting expression of diverse viewpoints and fostering an informed electorate. First, the provisions give broadcasters an incentive to cover all sides of an issue. If the broadcaster provides, from the start, an opportunity for all sides of the controversy to be heard, the provisions of the statute are neither administratively nor economically onerous.

Second, supporters argue that these provisions are effective in preventing domination of the broadcast media by those with the vast financial resources needed to buy broadcast time. Without the Fairness Doctrine, large corporations that hold particular views on a ballot proposition would be able to purchase advertisements, while groups with opposing viewpoints without funds for advertisements would not be heard. Similarly, without the statute, especially in those areas with few stations, broadcasters would be able to use their frequencies to further the political careers of favorite candidates by excluding opponents from the airwaves, thus influencing the outcome of elections. The current law is effective in preventing such one-sided election coverage.

Third, the effect Section 315 has on broadcasters' editorial decisions is not clear. Consequently, whether the statute has the inhibiting effect that the broadcasters contend it has is difficult to tell.[101] Many people argue that broadcasters need not feel inhibited because they are given wide discretion in covering important issues. They are not required to present every side of every controversial issue and are not required to present opposing views on topics that are merely newsworthy.

Fairness Doctrine advocates contend that any burden placed on broadcasters is minimal compared with the benefit that the public receives. Compliance with the rules constitutes a small portion of day-to-day operations of broadcasting stations, and severe action against violators is infrequent enough that broadcasters should not fear it. The majority of problems that arise are resolved at the local level between citizens and the local broadcaster.[102] One commentator has stated that the odds are less than one in one hundred that any given broadcast licensee in a year is going to get a letter from the FCC regarding a Fairness Doctrine complaint, and the odds are one in one thousand that in any given year a broadcaster will find an adverse action taken against it.[103] Supporters of the Fairness Doctrine contend that regulatory incentive for coverage of all sides of an issue will be more important in the future as FCC efforts to eliminate multiple ownership regulations increases the concentration of ownership of radio, television, and cable stations.

Is Section 315 Justified in the Absence of a Known Demand for Public Access to Many Viewpoints on Important Issues? Proponents of repealing Section 315 point out that no evidence shows that the demand for coverage of controversial issues of public importance would not be met without the mandate of Section 315. The First Amendment does not allow a government agency to determine that a particular kind of programming is in the public interest if in fact the public is indifferent; and the argument that the First Amendment requires Section 315 to protect access to a multitude of viewpoints is attenuated if a multitude of viewpoints is reasonably available through alternative technologies to broadcast such as cable. The question of whether demand exists, and whether it will be adequately met without the compulsion of Section 315, can perhaps best be answered by leaving the matter to marketplace forces.

Supporters of Section 315 point out that television coverage is the most widely available and most influential form of media coverage and that without Section 315 it is likely to be monopolized by those who can afford to buy airtime. Although other viewpoints may still be covered through other telecommunications outlets, that coverage will be far less effective, with the result that political power will gravitate toward television broadcasters. Broadcasters will be free to make in-kind contributions of editorial support to a favorite candidate while ignoring other candidates or showing them in a less favorable light. Stations would be free to sell all of their time to one nominee or one group or to support an initiative right before an election and influence the outcome of the election. Thus freedom from regulation could deprive the public of the benefit of vigorous debate.

APPENDIX

Section 315 of the Communications Act, 47 U.S.C. 315, Candidates for Public Office:

If any licensee shall permit any person who is a legally qualified candidate for any public office to use a broadcasting station, he shall afford equal opportunities to all other such candidates for that office in the use of such broadcasting station; *Provided,* That such licensee shall have no power of censorship over the material broadcast under the provisions of this section. No obligation is imposed under this subsection upon any licensee to allow the use of its station by any such candidate. Appearance by a legally qualified candidate on any —

1. bona fide newscast,
2. bona fide news interview,
3. bona fide news documentary (if the appearance of the candidate is incidental to the presentation of the subject or subjects covered by the news documentary), or
4. on-the-spot coverage of bona fide news events (including but not limited to political conventions and activities incidental thereto),

shall not be deemed to be use of a broadcasting station within the meaning of this subsection. Nothing in the foregoing sentence shall be construed as relieving broadcasters, in connection with the presentation of newscasts, news interviews, news documentaries, and on-the-spot coverage of news events, from the obligation imposed upon them under this chapter to operate in the public interest and to afford reasonable opportunity for the discussion of conflicting views on issues of public importance.

The charges made for the use of any broadcasting station by any person who is legally qualified for any public office in connection with his campaign for nomination for election, or election to such office shall not exceed —

1. during the forty-five days preceding the date of a primary or primary runoff election and during the sixty days preceding the date of a general or special election in which such person is a candidate, the lowest unit charge of the station for the same class and amount of time for the same period; and

2. at any other time, the charges made for comparable use of such station by other users thereof.

For purposes of this section —

1. the term "broadcasting station" includes a community antenna television system; and
2. the terms "licensee" and "station licensee" when used with respect to a community antenna television system mean the operator of such system.

The Commission shall prescribe appropriate rules and regulations to carry out the provisions of this section.

NOTES TO TEXT

1. In eliminating the programming guidelines, the commission noted that there has been an increasing amount of informational and total nonentertainment programming and that commercial television stations have been meeting the demand for such programming. Report and Order, MM Docket No. 83–670, 56 RR2d 1005, 1009–10 (1983). Although locally produced programming has declined, the commission found that stations were still devoting more time to local programming than the former FCC guidelines required. 56 RR2d at 1009–10.

2. The commission found that marketplace forces and not the FCC guidelines were keeping stations at below-guideline levels. Ibid., at 1026. Other considerations were the paperwork burden of record keeping, reviewing and monitoring guideline compliance, possible anticompetitive effects vis-à-vis other media, and concerns about the guidelines' chilling effect on commercial speech.

3. Instead, they need only submit quarterly lists describing five to ten issues to which the licensee gave particular attention with programming in the prior three months and a statement of how each issue was treated. Such a list is seen by the commission as an effective way to evaluate stations' public interest programming while reducing the burden on broadcasters to provide exhaustive logs. Ibid., at 1028–29.

4. By Policy Statement and Order released February 5, 1985, the commission eliminated policies concerning licensee distortion of audience ratings (47 C.F.R. §73.4040); conflict of interest (§73.4085) and sports announcer selection (§73.4245); promotion of nonbroadcast business of a station (§73.4225); and use of a station for personal advantage in other business activities; concert promotion announcements; failure to perform sales contracts; and false, misleading, and deceptive advertisements. See 50 *Federal Register* 5583, 5584 (1985). At the same time, the FCC issued its second Notice of Proposed Rulemaking concerning three additional business practices, fraudulent billing practices (§§73.4115 and 73.1205), network clipping (§§73.4155 and 73.1205), and combination advertising rates and joint sales practices (§73.4065). Additionally, the commission has deleted policies relating to distortion of audience ratings and use of inaccurate or exaggerated coverage maps by broadcast licensees and has deleted certain policies dealing with horse race programming and advertising. These changes are reviewed and summarized at 50 *Federal Register* 5584 (1985).

5. Report and Order, MM Docket No. 83–670, 56 RR2d at 1006.

6. Ibid., at 1007.

7. See E. Krasnow, L. Langley, and H. Terry, *The Politics of Broadcast Regulation* (New York: St. Martin's Press, 1982), pp. 10–16, for a discussion of the historical background of broadcast regulation.

8. National Broadcasting Co. v. United States, 319 U.S. 190, 211–12 (1943).

9. FCC News Release, May 15, 1985.

10. See Senate Committee on Commerce, Science, and Transportation, *Print and Electronics Media: The Case for First Amendment Parity,* 98th Congress, 1st session (Comm. print, 1983), p. 63.

11. R. Koppel, "The Applicability of the Equal Time Doctrine and the Reasonable Access Rule to Elections in the New Media Era," 40 Harv. J. Legis. 499, 512 (1983).

12. Freedom of Expression Act of 1983, Hearings before the Senate Committee on Commerce, Science, and Transportation, 98th Congress, 2d session (1984) (hereafter *1984 Hearings*) (statement of Dr. Robert S. Powers, Chief Scientist, FCC), p. 41.

13. National Cable Television Association, "Cable Television Developments" (February 1985).

14. Not everyone agrees that new communications media create a true condition of abundance. Some argue that scarcity still exists because demand far exceeds supply for a finite number of available frequencies, as reflected in the premium prices paid for license broadcast stations. Further, new forms of communications are not universally available and do not for the most part present controversial issues of public importance. See *1984 Hearings,* statement of Robert M. Gurss, Attorney, Media Access Project, p. 92.

15. 47 U.S.C. §307(c), formerly §307(d).

16. In an early case dealing with competing applications for a new station, the Supreme Court held that the grant of a license without a hearing to both applicants would deprive the loser of a legislatively mandated opportunity to contest the license award. Ashbacker Radio Corp. v. FCC, 326 U.S. 327 (1945). The Court also stated that license renewals for broadcasting stations are subject to the same considerations and practice which affect the granting of original applications. Ibid., at 332.

17. Responding to the quandary that broadcasters face when they must defend their own actual record in a comparison between that record and the promises of a challenger, the commission early made known that in a comparative hearing for an existing station between an incumbent licensee and a challenger, the past performance of the licensee is the most reliable indicator of future performance, even though the challenger fares better in a comparison of other factors. Hearst Radio, Inc. (WBAL), 15 FCC 1149 (1951).

18. See Central Florida Enterprises, Inc. v. FCC, 683 F.2d 503, 506 (D.C. Cir. 1982).

19. See, for example, FCC v. Pottsville Broadcasting Co., 309 U.S. 134 (1940); FCC v. Sanders Bros. Radio Station, 309 U.S. 470 (1940); National Broadcasting Co. v. United States, 319 U.S. 190 (1943).

20. National Broadcasting Co. v. United States, 319 U.S. at 215–16, citing 45 U.S.C. §303(g).

21. See National Broadcasting Co. v. United States, 319 U.S. at 215–16.

22. 395 U.S. 367 (1964).

23. 1 FCC2d 393, 5 RR2d 1901 (1965).

24. Seven League Productions, Inc., 1 FCC2d 1597 (1965).

25. WHDH, Inc., 16 FCC2d 1, recon. denied, 17 FCC2d 856 (1969), aff'd sub nom. Greater Boston Television Corp. v. FCC, 444 F.2d 841 (D.C. Cir. 1970), cert. denied, 403 U.S. 923 (1971).

26. 16 FCC2d at 10.

27. See Krasnow, Langley, and Terry, *Politics of Broadcast Regulation,* p. 209; see also Citizens' Communications Center v. FCC, 447 F.2d 1201, 1209 (D.C. Cir. 1971).

28. S.2004, 91st Congress, 1st session (1969).

29. *Policy Statement on Comparative Hearings Involving Regular Renewal Applicants,* 22 FCC2d 424, 18 RR2d 1901, recon. denied 24 FCC2d 383 (1970).

30. There were no formal rulemaking hearings and no opportunities to submit written arguments before the policy statement was issued. 24 FCC2d at 389.

31. Krasnow, Langley, and Terry, *Politics of Broadcast Regulation,* p. 216.

32. Citizens' Communications Center v. FCC, 447 F.2d 1201 (D.C. Cir. 1971).

33. 447 F.2d at 1213.

34. Senate Report 97–292, 97th Congress, 1st session (1981), p. 9.

35. Ibid.

36. Krasnow, Langley, and Terry, *Politics of Broadcast Regulation,* p. 220.

37. Broadcast Regulation Reform, Hearings before the House Committee on Energy and Commerce, 98th Congress, 1st session (1983) (hereafter *1983 Hearings*), p. 303.

38. Cowles Florida Broadcasting, Inc. 60 FCC2d 372, 37 RR2d 1487 (1976); 62 FCC2d 953, 955, 39 RR2d 541 (1977).

39. Central Florida Enterprises Inc. v. FCC, 598 F. 2d 37 (D.C. Cir. 1978).

40. Ibid. at 51.

41. 598 F.2d at 58–62.

42. Cowles Florida Broadcasting, Inc., 86 FCC2d 993 (1981).

43. Central Florida Enterprises, Inc. v. FCC, 683 F.2d 503 (D.C. Cir. 1982), cert. denied, 460 U.S. 1084 (1983).

44. H.R. 2382, 98th Congress, 1st session (1983) (Rep. Tauke, R-Iowa; Rep. Tauzin, D-La.). The bill had 235 cosponsors but did not get majority support on the Communications Subcommittee. *1984 Hearings* (testimony of Rep. Tauke, member, House Committee on Energy and Commerce), p. 267. See also S. 55, 98th Congress, 1st session (1983) (Sen. Barry Goldwater, R-Ariz.); H.R. 6122, 98th Congress, 2d session (1984) (Rep. Al Swift, D-Wash.; Rep. Timothy E. Wirth, D-Colo.; Rep. John D. Dingell, D-Mich.; Rep. Mickey Leland, D-Tex.; Rep. John Bryant, D-Tex.).

45. *1983 Hearings*, statement of Newton N. Minow, former chairman, FCC, pp. 44–48.

46. Because of the legislation that extended license terms from three to five years for television and three to seven years for radio, without staggering license renewals, no television licenses come up for renewal until October 1986, and no radio licenses come up for renewal until June 1988. In the absence of license renewals, there can be no petitions to deny. Members of the public may still express their dissatisfaction through formal or informal complaints to the commission, but there is no petition-to-revoke procedure whereby someone outside the commission may seek revocation of a license (although the commission can revoke a license on its own initiative). See *1983 Hearings*, testimony of James C. McKinney, chief, Mass Media Bureau, FCC, p. 287. Some commentators have suggested that a petition-to-revoke process might be made available in extraordinary circumstances (see *1983 Hearings*, testimony of Joel Chaseman, president, Post-Newsweek Stations, Inc., p. 141), but none of the bills introduced in the 98th or 99th Congresses contained such a provision.

47. According to news reports, a stalemate on the quantification question appears to be the main reason that no comparative renewal legislation was passed in the last Congress. See, for example, "TV Deregulation Bill Shelved," *Washington Post* (September 20, 1984).

48. *1983 Hearings*, testimony of Joel Chaseman, president, Post-Newsweek Stations, Inc., p. 141.

49. Senate Report 97–292, p. 11.

50. Ibid., pp. 13–14.

51. Ibid., p. 12. See also Hearings before the House Committee on Energy and Commerce on H.R. 6122, September 19, 1984, Statement of James C. McKinney, chief, Mass Media Bureau, FCC.

52. 1976 Report of the FCC to Congress re Comparative Renewal, paragraph 105, quoted in Senate Report 97–292, p. 11.

53. See *Congressional Record*, pp. S. 1289, S. 1291 (February 17, 1983).

54. *1983 Hearings*, testimony of Rep. W. J. Tauzin (D-La.), member, House Committee on Energy and Commerce, p. 295.

55. See note 24 above; see also in re Application of Simon Geller, 90 FCC2d 250, 51 RR2d 1019 (1982), recon. denied, 52 RR2d 709 (1982). This decision was upheld by the D.C. Circuit, Committee for Community Access v. FCC, 737 F.2d 74 (D.C. Cir. 1984), but the case was remanded to the commission so that the FCC could recalculate the comparative factors. Comments have been filed, and the case is pending.

56. *1984 Hearings*, statement of Charles D. Ferris, former chairman, FCC, p. 32.

57. Section 311(c)(3) provides that

> The Commission shall approve [a settlement] agreement only if it determines that (A) the agreement is consistent with the public interest, convenience, or necessity; and (B) no party to the agreement filed its application for the purpose of reaching or carrying out such agreement.

58. See *1983 Hearings*, testimony of Andrew Jay Schwartzman, executive director, Media Access Project, p. 299.

59. Ibid., p. 38.

60. *1984 Hearings*, p. 31.

61. See "We Sell Oil: Why Not the Spectrum?" *New York Times* (December 3, 1984). The FCC has proposed auction of spectrum space for uses other than mass media or public safety licenses. See "Revised FCC Fee Schedule Goes to Congress This Week; Auction Legislation in Works," *Communications Daily* (April 15, 1985), pp. 1–2.

62. The full text of Section 315 as amended is set out in the appendix. A history of the evolution of the Fairness Doctrine is contained in the FCC's Notice of Inquiry in General Docket No. 84-282 (Inquiry into Section 73.1910 of the Commission's Rules and Regulations Concerning the General Fairness Doctrine Obligations of Broadcast Licensees), released May 8, 1984.

63. See 47 C.F.R. §§73.1910 (Fairness Doctrine); 73.1920 (Personal attacks); 73.1930 (Political editorials); and 73.1940 (Broadcasts by candidates for public office). See also FCC Public Notice, "Fairness Doctrine and the Public Interest Standards," 39 *Federal Register* 26372 (1974); FCC Public Notice, "The Law of Political Broadcasting and Cablecasting," 43 *Federal Register* 32795 (1978). A current revised version of the latter notice is available from the FCC on request.

64. 47 C.F.R. §73.1940(a).

65. 47 C.F.R. §73.1940(b).

66. 47 C.F.R. §73.1940(b-d).

67. 47 C.F.R. §73.1940(g); see Section 312(a)(7) of the Communications Act, which provides the authority for this revocation.

68. Charles F. Dykas, 35 FCC2d 937 (1972).

69. A program about a candidate is a use if "the candidate's personal appearance is substantial in length, integrally involved in the program, and indeed the focus of the program; and when the program is under the control and direction of the candidate," the program constitutes a use. Gray Communications Systems, Inc., 14 FCC2d 766 (1968), recon. denied, 19 FCC2d 532 (1969).

70. Carter/Mondale Reelection Committee, 81 FCC2d 409 (1980); Letter to Mr. Nicholas Zapple, 23 FCC2d 707 (1970).

71. Debates, however, are exempt from the rule when it is clear that the broadcaster does not intend to give any candidate a political advantage. Thus a debate may be aired without the participation of all of the candidates for the office. Aspen Institute, 55 FCC2d 697 (1975) aff'd. sub. nom. Chisholm et al. v. FCC, 538 F.2d 349 (D.C. Cir. 1976), cert. denied, 97 S.Ct. 247 (1976).

72. 13 FCC 1246 (1949).

73. Ibid. at 1249.

74. Ibid.

75. Ibid. at 1256.

76. Mass Media Bureau Publication 8330-FD.

77. 39 *Federal Register* 26372, 26376 (1974).

78. Mass Media Bureau Publication 8330-FD, p. 3.

79. 39 *Federal Register* 26377.

80. See Brandywine-Main Line Radio, Inc. v. FCC, 473 F.2d 16, 35 (D.C. Cir. 1972), cert. denied, 412 U.S. 922 (1973).

81. Cullman Broadcasting Co., 40 FCC 576 (1963).

82. See Red Lion Broadcasting Co. v. FCC, 395 U.S. 367, 377–78 (1969).

83. The FCC has considered repeal or modification of these rules. See Repeal or Modification of the Personal Attack and Political Editorial Rules, Notice of Proposed Rule Making in Gen. Docket 83–484, 48 *Federal Register* 28295 (June 21, 1983).

84. 47 C.F.R. §73.1920.

85. 47 C.F.R. §73.1930.

86. *1984 Hearings,* statement of Craig R. Smith, president, Freedom of Expression Foundation.

87. See *Congressional Record* (daily ed., January 3, 1985), p. S. 108.

88. S. 22, §2, 99th Congress, 1st session (1985).

89. In the matter of inquiry into Section 73.1910 of the commission's Rules and Regulations concerning the general Fairness Doctrine's obligations of broadcast licensees, see General Document 84–282 at ¶100 (released May 8, 1984).

90. CBS Inc. v. FCC, 453 U.S. 367, 395 (1981), citing Red Lion, 395 U.S. at 390. See also C. Sheppard, "The Fairness Doctrine: Protection for a Scarce Public Resource," 14 St. Mary's L.J. 1083, 1085 (1983).

91. 395 U.S. at 390. See also, Time, Inc. v. Hill, 385 U.S. 374, 389 (1966).

92. There are, however, many exceptions; equal access and the Fairness Doctrine are only two among many. For instance, broadcast of indecent speech is prohibited, even though it may fall short of obscenity. See 18 U.S.C. §1464. Restrictions on commercial speech also exist and may be joined by a proposed legislative prohibition on liquor advertising.

93. 418 U.S. 241, 249–50 (1974).

94. See FCC v. Pacifica Foundation, 438 U.S. 726, 748 (1978), where the Court noted that "the broadcast media have established a uniquely pervasive presence in the lives of all Americans."

95. 376 U.S. 254, 279 (1964).

96. Ernest Schultz, executive vice-president of Radio and Television News Directors Association, AEI Conference on Government Regulation of the Media, unpublished transcript (March 21, 1983), p. 176.

97. In 1983, the commission exempted teletext from the Fairness Doctrine. 53 RR2d 1309, 1322–24.

98. See *1984 Hearings*, p. 210. The test, according to the FCC, is whether the advertisement "presents a meaningful statement which obviously addresses, and advocates a point of view on, the controversial issue of public importance." 48 FCC2d 23–24.

99. Ernest Schultz, AEI Conference on Government Regulation of the Media, p. 131.

100. 39 *Federal Register* 26384 (1974).

101. Compare, for example, testimony of Ford Rowan, attorney, appearing as a private citizen, *1984 Hearings*, p. 115, with testimony of Reed Irvine, Accuracy in the Media, *1984 Hearings*, p. 113. See also 39 *Federal Register* 26374, where the FCC states it has seen no credible evidence that the doctrines have in fact had the net effect of reducing rather than enhancing the volume and quality of coverage.

102. See Andrew Schwartzman, executive director, Media Access Project, AEI Conference on Government Regulation of the Media, p. 128.

103. Ibid., p. 129.

Selected AEI Publications

Regulation: The AEI Journal on Government and Society, published bimonthly (one year, $24; two years, $44; single copy, $5.00)

Review: 1984 Session of the Congress (1985, 76 pp., $4.95)

Proposed Procedures for a Limited Constitutional Convention (1984, 40 pp., $3.95)

Toxic Torts: Proposals for Compensating Victims of Hazardous Substances, (1984, 32 pp., $3.95)

Credit Controls: Should We Revive and Expand Them? (1984, 46 pp., $3.95)

Regulating Consumer Product Safety, W. Kip Viscusi (1984, 116 pp., cloth $14.95, paper $5.95)

Ethics-in-Government Laws: Are They Too "Ethical"? Alfred S. Neely IV (1984, 58 pp., $4.95)

The Regulation of Pharmaceuticals: Balancing the Benefits and Risks, Henry G. Grabowski and John M. Vernon (1983, 74 pp., $4.95)

The Political Economy of Deregulation: Interest Groups in the Regulatory Process, Roger G. Noll and Bruce M. Owen (1983, 164 pp., cloth $15.95, paper $7.95)

• *Mail orders for publications to:* AMERICAN ENTERPRISE INSTITUTE, 1150 Seventeenth Street, N.W., Washington, D.C. 20036 • *For postage and handling, add 10 percent of total; minimum charge $2, maximum $10 (no charge on prepaid orders)* • *For information on orders, or to expedite service, call toll free 800-424-2873 (in Washington, D.C., 202-862-5869)* • *Prices subject to change without notice.* • *Payable in U.S. currency through U.S. banks only*

AEI Associates Program

The American Enterprise Institute invites your participation in the competition of ideas through its AEI Associates Program. This program has two objectives: (1) to extend public familiarity with contemporary issues; and (2) to increase research on these issues and disseminate the results to policy makers, the academic community, journalists, and others who help shape public policies. The areas studied by AEI include Economic Policy, Education Policy, Energy Policy, Fiscal Policy, Government Regulation, Health Policy, International Programs, Legal Policy, National Defense Studies, Political and Social Processes, and Religion, Philosophy, and Public Policy. For the $49 annual fee, Associates receive

• a subscription to *Memorandum*, the newsletter on all AEI activities
• the AEI publications catalog and all supplements
• a 30 percent discount on all AEI books
• a 40 percent discount for certain seminars on key issues
• subscriptions to any two of the following publications: *Public Opinion*, a bimonthly magazine exploring trends and implications of public opinion on social and public policy questions; *Regulation*, a bimonthly journal examining all aspects of government regulation of society; and *AEI Economist*, a monthly newsletter analyzing current economic issues and evaluating future trends (or for all three publications, send an additional $12).

Call 202/862-6446 or write: AMERICAN ENTERPRISE INSTITUTE
1150 Seventeenth Street, N.W., Suite 301, Washington, D.C. 20036

The American Enterprise Institute for Public Policy Research, established in 1943, is a nonpartisan, nonprofit research and educational organization supported by foundations, corporations, and the public at large. Its purpose is to assist policy makers, scholars, business men and women, the press, and the public by providing objective analysis of national and international issues. Views expressed in the institute's publications are those of the authors and do not necessarily reflect the views of the staff, advisory panels, officers, or trustees of AEI.

Council of Academic Advisers

Paul W. McCracken, *Chairman, Edmund Ezra Day University Professor of Business Administration, University of Michigan*

*Kenneth W. Dam, *Harold J. and Marion F. Green Professor of Law, University of Chicago*

Donald C. Hellmann, *Professor of Political Science and International Studies, University of Washington*

D. Gale Johnson, *Eliakim Hastings Moore Distinguished Service Professor of Economics and Chairman, Department of Economics, University of Chicago*

Robert A. Nisbet, *Adjunct Scholar, American Enterprise Institute*

Herbert Stein, *A. Willis Robertson Professor of Economics Emeritus, University of Virginia*

Murray L. Weidenbaum, *Mallinckrodt Distinguished University Professor and Director, Center for the Study of American Business, Washington University*

James Q. Wilson, *Henry Lee Shattuck Professor of Government, Harvard University*

*On leave for government service.

Executive Committee

Richard B. Madden, *Chairman of the Board*
William J. Baroody, Jr., *President*
James G. Affleck

Willard C. Butcher
John J. Creedon
Paul F. Oreffice
Richard D. Wood

Tait Trussell,
 Vice President, Administration
Joseph J. Brady,
 Vice President, Development

Edward Styles, *Director of Publications*

Program Directors

Russell Chapin, *Legislative Analyses*
Denis P. Doyle, *Education Policy Studies*
Marvin Esch, *Seminars and Programs*
Thomas F. Johnson, *Economic Policy Studies*
Marvin H. Kosters,
 Government Regulation Studies

John H. Makin, *Fiscal Policy Studies*
Jack A. Meyer, *Health Policy Studies*
Michael Novak,
 Religion, Philosophy, and Public Policy
Howard R. Penniman/Austin Ranney,
 Political and Social Processes
Robert J. Pranger, *International Programs*

Periodicals

AEI Economist, Herbert Stein, *Ed.*

AEI Foreign Policy and Defense Review,
 Evron M. Kirkpatrick, Robert J.
 Pranger, and Harold H. Saunders, *Eds.*

Public Opinion, Seymour Martin
 Lipset and Ben J. Wattenberg, *Co-Eds.*,
 Everett Carll Ladd, *Sr. Ed.*,
 Karlyn H. Keene, *Mng. Ed.*

Regulation: AEI Journal on Government and Society, Anne Brunsdale, *Mng. Ed.*